W9-CPP-601

Experiments with Force and Motion

By Colin Uttley

Gareth Stevens
Publishing

Please visit our Web site www.garethstevens.com. For a free color catalog of all our high-quality books, call toll free 1-800-542-2595 or fax 1-877-542-2596.

Library of Congress Cataloging-in-Publication Data
Uttley, Colin.
    Experiments with force and motion / Colin Uttley.
       p. cm. -- (Cool science)
    Includes index.
    ISBN 978-1-4339-3459-9 (lib. bdg.) -- ISBN 978-1-4339-3460-5 (pbk.)
    ISBN 978-1-4339-3461-2 (6-pack)
    1. Force and energy--Experiments--Juvenile literature. 2. Motion--Experiments--Juvenile literature. I. Title.
QC73.4.U88 2010
531'.6--dc22
                            2009041580

Published in 2010 by
Gareth Stevens Publishing
111 East 14th Street, Suite 349
New York, NY 10003

© 2010 The Brown Reference Group Ltd.

For Gareth Stevens Publishing:
Art Direction: Haley Harasymiw
Editorial Direction: Kerri O'Donnell

For The Brown Reference Group Ltd:
Editorial Director: Lindsey Lowe
Managing Editor: Tim Harris
Editor: Sarah Eason
Children's Publisher: Anne O'Daly
Design Manager: David Poole
Designer: Paul Myerscough
Production Director: Alastair Gourlay

Picture Credits:
Front Cover: Shutterstock: Mano Photo (background); Ronen (foreground)
Title Page: Shutterstock: Mano Photo
Dreamtime.com: 7; NASA: 6t; Shutterstock: Joggie Botma 4, Willem Dijkstra 6b, Dan Simonsen 5
All other images Martin Norris

Publisher's note to educators and parents: Our editors have carefully reviewed the Web sites that appear on p. 31 to ensure that they are suitable for students. Many Web sites change frequently, however, and we cannot guarantee that a site's future contents will continue to meet our high standards of quality and educational value. Be advised that students should be closely supervised whenever they access the Internet.

Manufactured in the United States of America
1 2 3 4 5 6 7 8 9   12 11 10

CPSIA compliance information: Batch #BRW0102GS: For further information contact Gareth Stevens, New York, New York at 1-800-542-2595.

Contents

Introduction

Force and motion (movement) are inseparable. You cannot have one without the other. Forces make things move, change the way they move, and bring them to a stop. These forces act on everything in the universe, from the stars in the sky to the atoms that make up our bodies.

The world around us is constantly moving. Sometimes we can see this movement directly with our eyes. For example, clouds slowly move past in the sky, water flows downstream in a river, and your team mate might run past you on the football field. Other movement is not so clear. Everything might seem still when you are sitting in a quiet room. In fact, the atoms that make up the room and all the cells inside your body are constantly moving. The room is on a planet that spins as it orbits around the Sun.

A force called gravity makes this skydiver fall down to Earth when he jumps out of an airplane. As he falls, the flow of air around his body creates a force called drag, which slows him down.

Scientists have found out that the universe itself is on the move—it is expanding all the time. Forces are the cause of all this motion. The study of forces and motion is part of the science of physics.

Early ideas

Scientists have been studying forces and motion for thousands of years. In ancient Greece, philosopher Aristotle (384–322 BCE) came up with the idea of a "force" that pushed or pulled objects to move them. Aristotle understood how the force of his arm could throw a stone in the air. However, he could not explain why the stone kept on going when it left your hand, with no apparent force acting on it. Aristotle thought that as soon as the force was taken away the stone should stop moving.

In the seventeenth century, Italian scientist Galileo Galilei (1564–1642) started to do experiments to test his ideas about forces and motion. Galileo realized that when an object slows down or speeds up, it is because many different forces act on it. A stone is made to move by the force of a thrower's arm. As it moves through the air, the force of gravity pulls the stone toward the center of Earth. The stone is also slowed by a force called drag.

Galileo realized that without these forces slowing down moving objects and pulling them toward the ground, the objects would keep on moving in a straight line. He came up with the idea that objects change their speed only when a force acts on them. Galileo also suggested that an object keeps accelerating (speeding up) or decelerating (slowing down) as long as the forces acting on it do not cancel each other out.

LEARNING ABOUT SCIENCE

Doing experiments is the best way to learn about science. This is the way scientists test their ideas and find out new information. Follow this good science guide to get the most out of each experiment in this book.

• Never begin an experiment until you have talked to an adult about what you are going to do.
• Take care when you do or set up an experiment, whether it is dangerous or not. Make sure you know the safety rules before you start work. Wear goggles and use the right safety equipment when you are told to do so.
• Do each experiment more than once. The more times you carry out an experiment, the more accurate your results will be.
• Keep a notebook to record the results of your experiments. Make your results easy to read and understand. You can make notes and draw charts, diagrams, and tables.
• Drawing a graph is a great way of presenting your results. Plot the results of your experiment as dots on a graph. Use a ruler to draw a straight line through all the dots. Reading the graph will help you to fill in the gaps in your experiment.
• Write down the results as you do each experiment. If one result seems different from the rest, you might have made a mistake that you can fix immediately.
• Learn from your mistakes. Some of the most exciting findings in science came from an unexpected result. If your results do not tally with your predictions, try to find out why.

Fighter pilots feel some extreme forces when they fly jet planes. G-force is the force equal to Earth's gravity. On Earth, a person feels a force of 1G. Pilots feel up to 9G during steep climbs and dives.

Newton's laws of motion

Building on the ideas of Galileo, English scientist Isaac Newton (1642–1727) came up with three basic laws to explain how forces control the motion of objects. The most amazing thing about Newton's laws is that they can be used to explain the movement of almost all objects, from the way our planet moves around the Sun to the way a ball moves through the air.

Newton's first law says that if an object is not pushed or pulled by a force, it will stay still or keep moving in a straight line at a constant speed. For example, a rocket on a launch pad will sit still until the engines fire and force it upward. This tendency of objects to stay still or keep going is called inertia. In the emptiness of space, inertia can make a spacecraft carry on moving forever at the same speed unless the engine is used to slow it down or speed it up, or the spacecraft bumps into something.

MIGHTY MACHINES

People have been using simple machines for thousands of years. Simple machines include gears, levers, pulleys, and ramps. They increase the size of the force you exert to make jobs much easier. For example, levers help us crack open hard nuts and cut paper using scissors. Pulleys help us lift heavy loads. Gears change the direction of forces. For example, they convert the up-and-down movement of a piston in an engine into the turning movement of a car's wheels.

Newton's three laws of motion are the basic science that was used to send the Apollo 11 astronauts to the Moon.

Newton's second law of motion explains how an object either speeds up or slows down when a force acts on it. The change of speed, called acceleration (a), depends on the size of the force (F) and the object's mass (m). The law is summed up in the following equation:

$$F = ma$$
force = mass × acceleration

Mass is the amount of matter an object contains. A truck is more massive than a car, so a bigger force is needed to make it speed up or slow down.

Newton's third law says that every action has an equal, opposite reaction. (Newton used the words *action* and *reaction* instead of force.) This is how a rocket works. The blast of burning gas from the rocket's engine is the action. The rocket taking off is the reaction.

The experiments in this book are all safe if you follow the instructions very carefully in each one. If you are ever in any doubt about what to do, ask an adult to help you.

Twentieth-century ideas

Newton's laws describe the movement of most objects but the laws do not work very well for the motion of tiny particles inside atoms. German scientist Max Planck (1858–1947) solved this problem by developing quantum theory. Nor do they work for objects moving very quickly. German-born U.S. scientist Albert Einstein (1879–1955) came up with an idea called relativity in 1905 to describe the movement of things that travel close to the speed of light—186,000 miles (300,000km) per hour. Using relativity, Einstein showed that the mass of an object actually increases as it moves faster through space. At speeds much lower than the speed of light, this change in mass is not very noticeable. That is why Newton's laws work well in most everyday situations.

All about energy

Every time you ride a bicycle, you use energy to move. Scientists use the term *kinetic energy* to describe the energy of moving objects. The faster or heavier a moving object is, the more kinetic energy it has. So a jumbo jet has far more kinetic energy than you riding your bike, because it is much heavier and faster. Objects do not have to be moving to contain energy. If you push a bicycle up a hill, you can ride back down without pedaling. You have given the bicycle a type of energy called *potential energy*, which means it has the potential to move when you let it go.

When you use energy, it does not disappear. It changes from one form into another. The potential energy in a bicycle at the top of a hill changes into kinetic energy as you cycle downhill. To stop the bike, you need to get rid of the kinetic energy. The brakes can do this by creating friction. They rub against the wheel rims and turn the kinetic energy into heat energy and sound energy.

Fundamental forces

Scientists think that there are four fundamental forces in the universe. They are gravity, electromagnetism, strong nuclear force, and weak nuclear force. Gravity is the force of attraction between different masses. It keeps your feet firmly on the ground and Earth in orbit around the Sun. Electromagnetism holds atoms and molecules together. It is stronger than gravity but acts over a shorter distance. Strong and weak nuclear forces exist only in the middle of atoms. These forces are much stronger than gravity and electromagnetism. Scientists have unleashed the power of these forces to devastating effect by creating the atomic bomb.

Particle accelerators

Scientists hope to answer some of their questions about how the universe was created by smashing atoms together inside particle accelerators. The world's biggest particle accelerator is the Large Hadron Collider at the European Organization for Nuclear Research (CERN), on the French–Swiss border. It is 17 miles (27km) long and is buried 570 feet (174m) underground.

Scientists search for answers about the universe using particle accelerators such as the Large Hadron Collider, shown here.

Jet Boat

Goals

1 Build your own jet boat.

2 Investigate Newton's laws of motion.

3 Find out how drag slows down your jet boat.

LEVEL of Difficulty   Hard   Medium   Easy

What you will need

- 3-inch (7.5-cm) length of plastic tubing, or a straw that can bend without breaking
- rubber stopper with a hole in it
- small, flat piece of Styrofoam
- balloons of different sizes
- bath, pond, or wading pool for your jet boat to zoom across!

1 Push the plastic tube into the stopper.

SAFETY TiP!

If you do not have a rubber stopper with a hole, you can use a cork. Cutting a hole in a cork can be tricky, so ask an adult to do it for you. Remember that it is easier to cut the cork in half first to make it shorter.

2 Push the free end of the tube through the end of the Styrofoam tray. The tray will be the body of your boat.

WHOOSH!

A few high-speed boats use a jet engine like the one you have made. The fastest travel at 320 miles (515km) per hour. Most boats use propellers for power instead. The propellers whizz around, pulling water from under the boat and pushing it to the back.

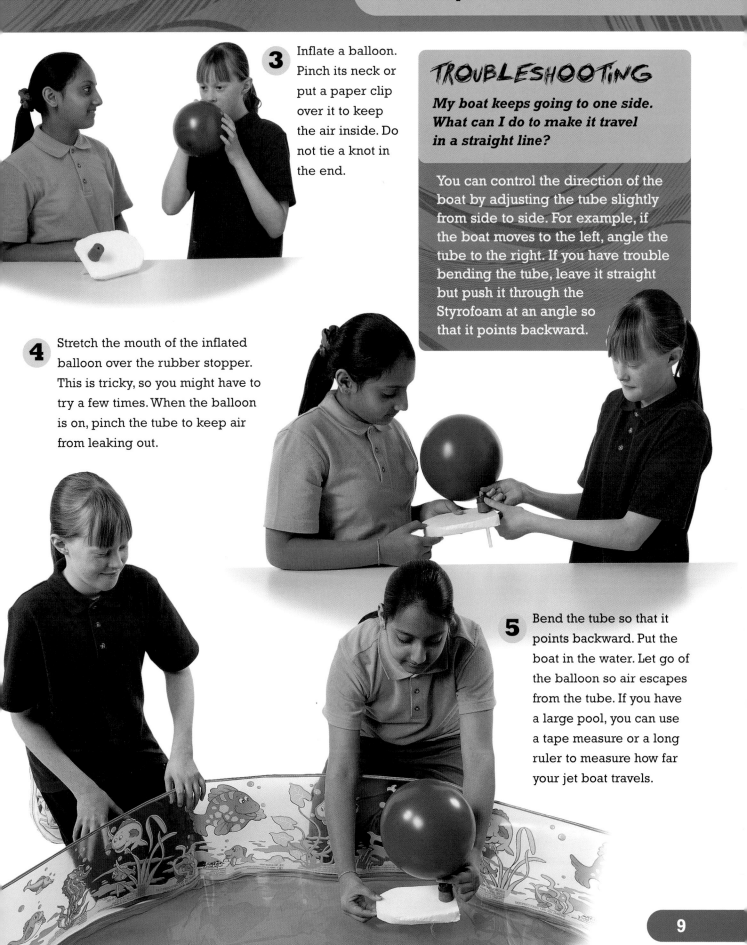

3 Inflate a balloon. Pinch its neck or put a paper clip over it to keep the air inside. Do not tie a knot in the end.

TROUBLESHOOTING

My boat keeps going to one side. What can I do to make it travel in a straight line?

You can control the direction of the boat by adjusting the tube slightly from side to side. For example, if the boat moves to the left, angle the tube to the right. If you have trouble bending the tube, leave it straight but push it through the Styrofoam at an angle so that it points backward.

4 Stretch the mouth of the inflated balloon over the rubber stopper. This is tricky, so you might have to try a few times. When the balloon is on, pinch the tube to keep air from leaking out.

5 Bend the tube so that it points backward. Put the boat in the water. Let go of the balloon so air escapes from the tube. If you have a large pool, you can use a tape measure or a long ruler to measure how far your jet boat travels.

On a Roll!

What you will need

- 2 identical cylinders such as metal cans with resealable lids
- circular metal weights such as metal washers or coins
- sticky tape
- wooden board about 3 feet (1m) long

Goals

1 Change potential energy into kinetic energy.

2 Find out how the distribution of weight affects the motion of a spinning object.

LEVEL of Difficulty

 Hard   Medium   Easy

SAFETY TiP!

Take care not to trap your fingers in the heavy books when you set up your ramp.

1 Tape 6 weights to the curved inside surface of the first cylinder (not on the lid or the bottom of the cylinder). Tape 3 weights near the open end of the cylinder and 3 near the bottom.

2 Tape 3 weights inside the second cylinder, right in the middle at the bottom. It might help to tape the weights together first. Tape another stack of 3 weights on the underside of the lid. Put the lids back on both cylinders.

3 Use some heavy books to prop up one end of the wooden board to about 12 inches (30cm) high.

4 Let the cylinders roll down the ramp. Figure out the best place to release them so they don't roll off the edge or bump into each other.

5 Time the cylinders as they roll down the ramp. Make sure they start from the same place.

TROUBLESHOOTING

The cylinders run down the ramp too quickly to time them. How can I slow them down?

Just let the cylinders roll down—don't push them. Also lower the angle of the ramp. The cylinders will then roll slower, giving you more time to watch them move. The cylinders do not have to roll at top speed—you are only interested in how they gain speed in relation to each other.

Human Gyroscope

Goals

1 Turn yourself into a human gyroscope.

2 Learn about the forces that affect spinning objects.

LEVEL of Difficulty   Hard   Medium   Easy

What you will need

- bicycle wheel
- rubber stoppers or corks
- swivel chair that moves easily
- a friend to help you

1 Hold a bicycle wheel by the axles (the metal rods that join the wheel to the bicycle). If they are too small, use corks or rubber stoppers to make small handles.

2 Sit on the swivel chair with your feet on the ground. Ask friend to spin the wheel while you hold it. Take care not to get any fingers caught in the spokes.

SPINNING SATELLITES

Some satellites act like large gyroscopes. They are put into a deliberate spin so they are less likely to drift off course as they orbit Earth. The satellites that beam phone calls around the world have to stay over the exact same place all the time. They contain spinning disks called momentum wheels that fine-tune the satellite's position. Speeding up or slowing down the momentum wheel keeps the satellite in position.

AUTOPILOT

Gyroscopes help pilots fly long distances. Every airliner is equipped with an autopilot that keeps it flying along the course selected by the pilots. At the heart of the autopilot is a gyroscope that always points in the same direction. If the plane goes off course, the gyroscope detects this movement. The autopilot can then bring the plane back on course without the pilot having to do anything.

TROUBLESHOOTING

I tried the experiment, but the chair didn't move. What is going wrong?

Your chair is probably too stiff. Ask an adult to put oil on the chair's bearings or try another chair. Or ask someone to give the chair a push to get you going at the start. Spinning the wheel more quickly would help and so would a bigger wheel. But make sure you can still hold the wheel comfortably.

3 With the wheel held upright, lift your feet. Then tilt the wheel. What happens to the chair?

SAFETY TIP!

BEWARE! This experiment can be dangerous. When the wheel is spinning quickly, it will be hard to stop. Never put your fingers in the spokes or grip the tire with your hand. The friction will create heat energy that burns your skin! To stop the wheel, let it rub on the ground—you'll see how much friction it can cause.

Pendulum Painter

What you will need

- plastic cup
- hole punch
- string
- pin
- masking tape
- water-based paint
- newspaper
- large sheet of paper

Goals

1 Build a compound pendulum.

2 Study the swinging motion of your pendulum.

3 Use your pendulum to create amazing paint patterns.

LEVEL of Difficulty

 Hard   Medium   Easy

1 Make three holes around the rim of the cup with a hole punch. Tie a 3-inch (7.6-cm) length of string through each hole. Knot these strings together above the cup. Tie them to the end of a 1-foot (30-cm) length of string.

SAFETY TIP!

Use only water-based paint with this activity. If you make a mess, it will be easy to clean up.

2 Make a small hole in the bottom of the plastic cup with a pin. Cover the hole with a piece of tape.

3 Tie a long piece of string between two walls so that it runs above a table. Tie the string on the cup to the long piece of string. The cup needs to hang over the middle of the table.

5 Pull the cup to one side, peel off the tape, and then let go of the cup. As the cup swings, the paint will dribble out and make a pattern on the paper.

4 Cover the table with newspaper. Put a large piece of plain paper directly under the cup. Put paint in the cup.

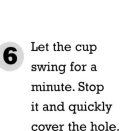

6 Let the cup swing for a minute. Stop it and quickly cover the hole.

TROUBLESHOOTING

What if I can't hang the cup over a table?

Work on the floor. Position two chairs, back to back, 2 feet (61cm) apart. Put heavy books on the seats. Tie the pendulum to the chair tops.

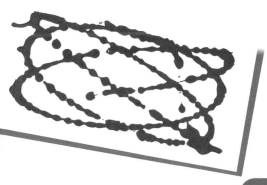

Twin Pendulums

Goals

1 Build a pair of resonating pendulums.

2 Make a pendulum move without touching it.

LEVEL of Difficulty

 Hard   Medium   Easy

What you will need

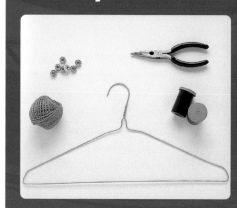

- metal coat hanger
- wire cutters
- hole punch
- film canisters
- metal nuts of the same size to use as weights
- string

1 Cut two lengths of wire from the coat hanger, each about 6 inches (15cm) long. Use the wire cutters to bend one end of each wire into a loop.

SAFETY TiP !

Take care when cutting the wire. Small pieces of wire can fly off and hit you in the eye. Wear safety goggles if you have them (or sunglasses if you don't). The ends of the wire are sharp, so take care not to cut your fingers. A hole punch is the safest way to make holes in the lids of the film canisters.

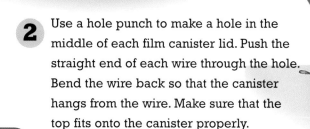

2 Use a hole punch to make a hole in the middle of each film canister lid. Push the straight end of each wire through the hole. Bend the wire back so that the canister hangs from the wire. Make sure that the top fits onto the canister properly.

3 Put the same number of nuts in each canister. Put the lids on the canisters.

SMOOTH RIDE

Automobiles have springs to smooth out the ride on bumpy roads. When a wheel hits a rut in the road, the spring can start to vibrate at its natural frequency. This makes the ride very bouncy. To overcome this problem, cars are fitted with shock absorbers. One type of shock absorber is a cylinder filled with fluid, which has a disk inside. The disk moves up and down smoothly, absorbing the energy of sudden, juddering jolts.

4 Cut a piece of string about 2 feet (60cm) long. Tie it between two chairs or from wall to wall so that it is taught. Hang the wires over the string so that they are at equal distances from the center of the string, about 4 inches (10cm) apart.

TROUBLESHOOTING

How can I stop the canisters from sliding together when I swing the pendulum?

Tie the string tighter so that it doesn't sag. That will stop the canisters from sliding together. You could space them a little bit farther apart, too.

5 Pull back one of the canisters, let go, and allow it to swing. Watch what happens to the other pendulum.

Bend and Bow

What you will need

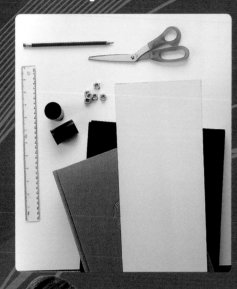

- ruler
- pencil
- card
- scissors
- heavy books to make two piles of the same height
- film canisters
- metal washers or coins to use as weights

Goals

1 Build a beam bridge.

2 Test the strength of your beam bridge.

LEVEL of Difficulty

 Hard   Medium   Easy

SAFETY TIP!
Take care when using scissors. Always cut away from your body.

1 Use a ruler and pencil to measure and mark out a strip of card 22 inches (55cm) long and 2 inches (5cm) wide.

2 Cut out the strip. Use a ruler to find the halfway point along one long side. Mark this point with a pencil.

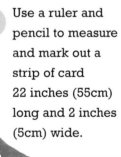

GALLOPING GERTIE

Sometimes bridge designers make serious mistakes. The Tacoma Narrows Bridge was a suspension bridge built across a stretch of water called the Narrows of Puget Sound in Washington State. It was nicknamed "Galloping Gertie" because it used to flex in the wind. On November 7, 1940, the bridge twisted so much that it collapsed into the water, taking with it a dog abandoned in a car.

BETTER TO BEND

Flying through turbulence can be a frightening experience. The wings of an airplane move up and down in the bumpy air, which is exactly what they are designed to do. If engineers tried to build wings that did not bend, they would have to be very thick and heavy. It is much better to allow them to bend. Bridges are also designed to sway and bend a little in the wind.

3 Make two piles of books 18 inches (45cm) apart. Put the card strip between the books to make a bridge.

TROUBLESHOOTING

What if my bridge sags too easily or doesn't sag at all?

Use the right thickness of card. Thick corrugated card is very strong and will hold a lot of weight without sagging. Very thin card won't hold enough weight for the experiment to work properly.

4 Put the canister in the middle of the bridge. Put a weight in the canister, and measure how much the bridge sags—the distance from the table to the center of the bridge.

5 Keep adding weights until the bridge collapses or touches the ground. Measure the sagging distance each time you add a weight.

Building a Ramp

Goals

1 Find out why less force is needed to lift a load when a ramp is used.

2 Learn about mechanical advantage.

LEVEL of Difficulty

 Hard   Medium   Easy

What you will need

- hole punch
- film canister
- piece of elastic or some rubber bands
- metal nuts or coins
- ruler
- books
- wooden board or piece of plastic 2 feet (61cm) long

1 Make a hole in the lid of the film canister with a hole punch. Thread the elastic through the hole, and tie a knot in it so that it does not slip out.

ROUND RAMP

A screw has a thread that spirals around it from one end to the other. When someone turns the screw with a screwdriver, the thread acts like a ramp, moving into the wood with a greater force than is used to turn it.

SAFETY TIP!

Ask an adult to make a hole in the lid if you don't have a hole punch.

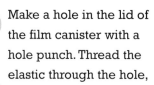

2 Put some metal nuts or coins in the bottom of the canister. Click the lid back on.

3 Measure the length of the elastic without stretching it.

TROUBLESHOOTING

What if the elastic doesn't stretch enough to measure?

Some types of elastic are not very stretchy. Use a rubber band if your elastic does not stretch very much. Cut the rubber band to make one long piece. To stop it from pulling through the hole, tie one end around a toothpick and then push the other end through the hole in the lid.

4 Use the elastic to lift the weight up to the height of a stack of books. Measure the length of the elastic.

5 Rest the wooden board or piece of plastic on the books to make a ramp.

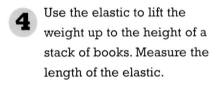

6 Use the elastic to pull the weight up the ramp. Measure the length of the elastic as it pulls the weight. You should find that the elastic doesn't stretch as much as when no ramp was used. This is a simple example of mechanical advantage.

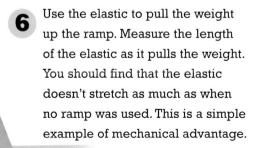

Making a Lever

What you will need

- 2 rulers, 12 inches (30cm) long
- 24 matchsticks
- sticky tape
- 4 books
- 2 film canisters
- metal nuts or coins
- modeling clay

Goals

1 Make a simple lever.

2 Explore how the lever magnifies force.

LEVEL of Difficulty

 Hard   Medium   Easy

IMPROVISED LEVER

In 1947, U.S. pilot Chuck Yeager (1923–) flew faster than the speed of sound in his rocket-powered airplane Bell X-1. The day before his flight, Yeager was thrown from his horse and broke his ribs. He found it impossible to close the airplane's hatch—until he attached a broom handle to it, making a long lever.

1 Draw lines on one of the rulers, 1 inch (2.5cm) apart. Tape pairs of matchsticks next to each mark. Each pair should be 0.13 inch (3mm) apart. The matchsticks will stop your lever from slipping.

2 Use the second ruler to make a platform for your lever. Wedge the ruler between four books.

SAFETY TIP !

Use safety matches so there is less chance of starting a fire.

3 Take two pieces of modeling clay of the same size. Put each piece on the bottom of a film canister. Stick one canister to each end of the lever on the side without any matchsticks.

4 Use metal nuts or coins as weights. Put two weights in one canister and four in the other. You are going to try to raise the heavier weight (the load) with the lighter weight (the effort), using your lever to help you.

TROUBLESHOOTING

The film canisters keep falling off each time I lift up the lever to move it.

Use a larger piece of modeling clay to keep the canisters in place, but make sure you use the same size under each canister. Otherwise the weight of the clay would affect the experiment. If you are worried that one piece is heavier than the other, weigh them using kitchen scales.

5 Put the lever on the platform. It won't balance at first, so adjust the position of the lighter weight until it does. Write down the position of the fulcrum (where the rulers touch) and the distances between the fulcrum and the weights. Repeat the activity, each time moving the lever up one matchstick-notch on the ruler.

Pulling with a Pulley

Goals

1 Make a pulley system.

2 Reduce the force needed to lift a load.

LEVEL of Difficulty

 Hard Medium Easy

What you will need

- compass
- pencils
- sheet of thick card
- glue
- 2 small plastic cups
- hole punch
- string
- wooden dowel
- 2 chairs
- metal washers or coins
- notebook

1 Use a compass to draw three circles on the card. Two circles should have a diameter of 2 inches (5cm), so the distance between the pencil and the compass point must be 1 inch (2.5cm). The other circle should be 1.6 inches (4cm) wide—move your compass apart 0.8 inches (2cm).

2 Glue the circles together, with the small circle between the two large circles. You have made a pulley wheel. Put a weight on top of the pulley wheel as it dries so that it bonds well.

PULLED FREE

Off-road vehicles can get stuck in mud. That is why many of them have a built-in winch. When it is obvious that the wheels alone cannot move the vehicle, the driver takes the cable from the winch and fastens it to a tree. The winch, driven by the engine, uses something called a compound-pulley system to haul the vehicle free.

3 Ask an adult to help you pierce a hole through the center of the wheel. Push a pencil through the hole.

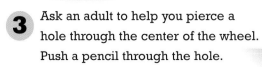

4 Make two holes near the top of each plastic cup. Tie a short piece of string between the holes.

5 Use two lengths of string to hang the pulley from the dowel. Balance the dowel between two chairs so it is off the ground. Put a long piece of string over the pulley wheel so that it hangs down on both sides. Tie one cup to one end of the string.

SAFETY TiP!

Cutting thick card can be difficult. Ask an adult to help you if you have any problems. Use a hole punch to make holes in the cups safely.

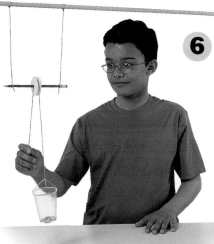

6 Put a few metal washers or coins in the cup. Pull down on the string. Notice how much effort it takes to lift the weight.

TROUBLESHOOTING

What should I do if the pulley keeps on getting stuck and does not move freely?

If the pulley wheel does not move smoothly, you will need to make the pencil hole a little bigger so that the pulley wheel can turn more easily.

7 Tie the second cup to the other end of the string. Put several weights in one of the cups. Add metal washers or coins to the other cup until the first cup rises. Make a note of how many weights are in each cup.

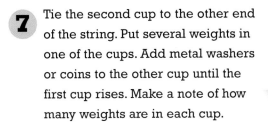

Weighing Water

What you will need

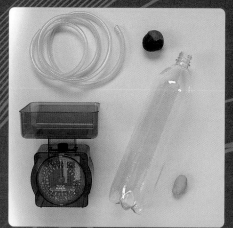

- 2 pieces of modeling clay
- weighing scales with container or a separate bowl
- large plastic soda bottle
- plastic tubing

Goals

1. Show that an object displaces water in a container.
2. Compare the weight of the displaced water and the weight of the object.

LEVEL of Difficulty

Hard   Medium   Easy

1 Put the empty container on the scale. Set the scale to read zero. Take a large piece of clay, and weigh it.

SAFETY TIP!

It is best to ask an adult to make the holes in the container for you.

2 Ask an adult to cut the top off a large plastic soda bottle. Make a hole in the side just above halfway up. Put a piece of plastic tubing through the hole.

3 Seal around the plastic tubing using a piece of modeling clay. This will stop water from leaking out around the edges.

4 Put the tube into the container to catch the overflow. Pour water into the bottle until it reaches the bottom of the tube but does not flow out of the tube.

DOUBLE DENSITY

Submarines move up and down through the water by changing their density. Submarines are built with two hulls—one inside the other. The main hull is always filled with air. This is the part of the submarine that contains the crew, engines, and equipment. The other hull, outside the main hull, can be filled with air or water. Water in the hull makes the submarine sink. When the water is replaced by air, the submarine rises to the surface of the water.

6 Weigh the container with the water in it. Because you set the scale to zero with the container on top, the scales now show the weight of the water only. Repeat the experiment with different objects—use some that float and some that sink.

5 Put the piece of modeling clay into the water. Water will flow out through the tube and into the container.

Blowing Bubbles

Goals

1 See how water molecules are attracted to each other in a film of soap.

LEVEL of Difficulty

 Hard   Medium   Easy

What you will need

- water
- tablespoon
- teaspoon
- dishwashing liquid
- bowl
- glycerol or corn syrup
- plastic plate
- drinking straws
- pipe cleaners

1 Put 10 tablespoons of water into a bowl. Add one tablespoon of dishwashing liquid.

2 Add one teaspoon of glycerol or corn syrup to the bowl. Stir the mixture.

3 Transfer a few tablespoons of the bubble solution onto the plastic plate.

SOAP

Grease forms stubborn stains on our clothes, the floor, and even our skin. By itself, water is not a good cleaning agent because water molecules and grease molecules repel one another. Soaps are excellent cleaning agents. Soap is made from animal or vegetable fats mixed with other chemicals. One end of a soap molecule is attracted to water. The other end of the same molecule is attracted to the grease. When we make a soapy lather, soap and water molecules stick to the grease molecules. The grease and soap can then be washed away with more water.

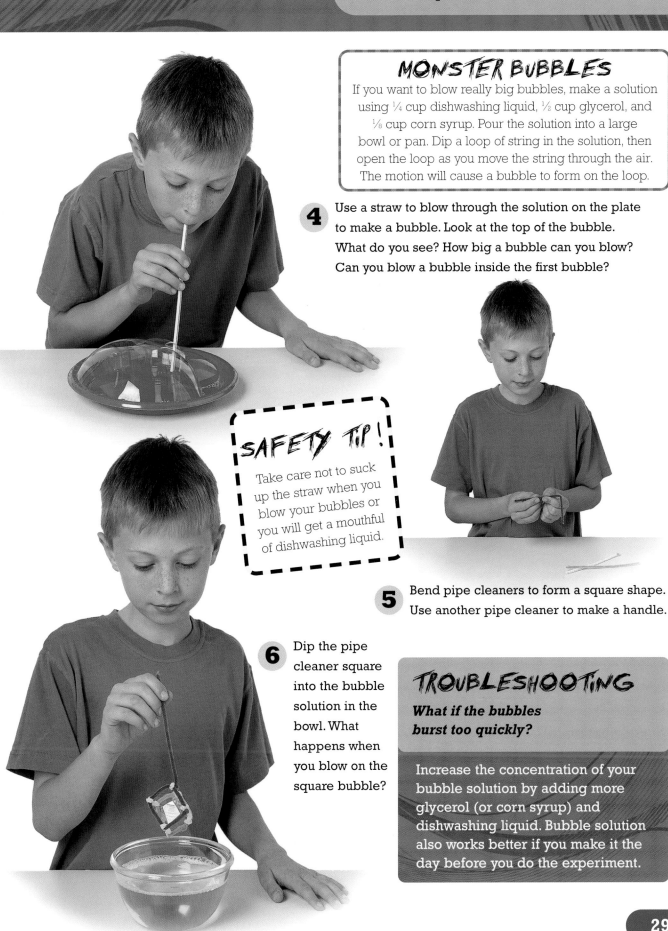

MONSTER BUBBLES

If you want to blow really big bubbles, make a solution using ¼ cup dishwashing liquid, ½ cup glycerol, and ⅛ cup corn syrup. Pour the solution into a large bowl or pan. Dip a loop of string in the solution, then open the loop as you move the string through the air. The motion will cause a bubble to form on the loop.

4 Use a straw to blow through the solution on the plate to make a bubble. Look at the top of the bubble. What do you see? How big a bubble can you blow? Can you blow a bubble inside the first bubble?

SAFETY TIP!

Take care not to suck up the straw when you blow your bubbles or you will get a mouthful of dishwashing liquid.

5 Bend pipe cleaners to form a square shape. Use another pipe cleaner to make a handle.

6 Dip the pipe cleaner square into the bubble solution in the bowl. What happens when you blow on the square bubble?

TROUBLESHOOTING

What if the bubbles burst too quickly?

Increase the concentration of your bubble solution by adding more glycerol (or corn syrup) and dishwashing liquid. Bubble solution also works better if you make it the day before you do the experiment.

Glossary

accelerate: to move faster

atoms: the tiny building blocks of all objects

density: the mass of an object in a given volume

drag: a force that pushes against something when it moves

electromagnetism: a magnetic force produced by the flow of electricity

energy: the ability of something to make things happen. For example, a ball moving through the air has energy because it could smash a window.

force: a push or pull on an object

friction: a force that stops something from moving

gear: a simple machine that helps control the speed or direction of a moving object

gravity: the force of attraction between different masses

gyroscope: a rotating wheel that can spin freely in all directions

inertia: the tendency of a stationary object to stay still, or a moving object to keep on going

jet engine: an engine that burns fuel to create a stream of hot gas that pushes an object, such as a jet plane, forward

kinetic energy: the energy of a moving object

lever: a bar that pivots around a point called the fulcrum to move a load

liquid: one of the states of matter. Liquids have a fixed volume but no shape, so they take the shape of their container.

mass: the amount of matter that an object contains

molecules: a group of atoms joined together by chemical bonds

particle accelerator: a machine that smashes particles together at very high speeds to find out about the forces that hold atoms together

pendulum: an object that hangs from a fixed point and is free to swing

potential energy: the energy of an object due to its position

propeller: a metal disk with blades that spin around to push a vehicle through the air or water

pulley: a rope-and-wheel system that helps people lift heavy loads

relativity: a theory that describes the forces acting on objects moving close to the speed of light

satellite: an object that orbits another in space. Natural satellites include the Moon; artificial satellites include communications and weather satellites.

speed: the distance traveled in a given time

speed of light: 186,000 miles (300,000km) per second

Styrofoam: a very light plastic filled with air bubbles

turbulence: when air or a liquid swirls around the surface of a moving object and slows it down

weight: the force of gravity pushing down on an object

Further Information

BOOKS

DiSpezio, Michael A. *Awesome Experiments in Force & Motion.* New York: Sterling, 2006.

Royston, Angela. *Forces and Motion.* Mankato, MN: Heinemann-Raintree, 2008.

Solway, Andrew. *Exploring Forces and Motion.* New York: Rosen Publishing, 2007.

Spilsbury, Richard, and Louise Spilsbury. *What Are Forces and Motion?* Berkeley Heights, NJ: Enslow Elementary, 2008.

Tocci, Salvatore. *Experiments with Motion.* New York: Children's Press, 2003.

WEB SITES

www.physics4kids.com/files/motion_intro.html

www.usoe.k12.ut.us/CURR/Science/sciber00/8th/forces/sciber/forcmot.htm

Index